ESSENTIAL SONGS FOR

viola

Available for
FLUTE, CLARINET, ALTO SAX, TENOR SAX, TRUMPET,
HORN, TROMBONE, VIOLIN, VIOLA, CELLO

ISBN 978-1-4234-5539-4

HAL•LEONARD®
CORPORATION
7777 W. BLUEMOUND RD. P.O. BOX 13819 MILWAUKEE, WI 53213

Visit Hal Leonard Online at
www.halleonard.com

CONTENTS

ALL SHOOK UP

VIOLA

Words and Music by OTIS BLACKWELL
and ELVIS PRESLEY

ALL THE WAY
from THE JOKER IS WILD

VIOLA

Words by SAMMY CAHN
Music by JAMES VEN HEUSEN

AND I LOVE HER

VIOLA

Words and Music by JOHN LENNON
and PAUL McCARTNEY

ANYONE CAN WHISTLE
from ANYONE CAN WHISTLE

VIOLA

Words and Music by
STEPHEN SONDHEIM

Slowly and tenderly

AUTUMN LEAVES

VIOLA

English lyrics by JOHNNY MERCER
French lyrics by JACQUES PREVERT
Music by JOSEPH KOSMA

Slowly, with expression

BABY, I LOVE YOUR WAY

VIOLA

Words and Music by
PETER FRAMPTON

BACK AT ONE

VIOLA

Words and Music by
BRIAN McKNIGHT

BEAUTIFUL

VIOLA

Words and Music by
LINDA PERRY

BECAUSE OF YOU

VIOLA

Words and Music by KELLY CLARKSON,
DAVID HODGES and BEN MOODY

BENNIE AND THE JETS

VIOLA

Words and Music by ELTON JOHN
and BERNIE TAUPIN

BLESS THE BROKEN ROAD

VIOLA

Words and Music by MARCUS HUMMON,
BOBBY BOYD and JEFF HANNA

D.S. al Coda

CODA

BORN FREE

from the Columbia Pictures' Release BORN FREE

VIOLA

Words by DON BLACK
Music by JOHN BARRY

BRING HIM HOME
from *LES MISÉRABLES*

Viola

Music by CLAUDE-MICHEL SCHÖNBERG
Lyrics by ALAIN BOUBLIL and HERBERT KRETZMER

BREATHE

VIOLA

Words and Music by HOLLY LAMAR
and STEPHANIE BENTLEY

Moderately fast

BYE BYE LOVE

VIOLA

Words and Music by FELICE BRYANT
and BOUDLEAUX BRYANT

CALIFORNIA GIRLS

VIOLA

Words and Music by BRIAN WILSON
and MIKE LOVE

CAN YOU FEEL THE LOVE TONIGHT

from Walt Disney Pictures' THE LION KING

VIOLA

Music by ELTON JOHN
Lyrics by TIM RICE

THE CHICKEN DANCE

VIOLA

By TERRY RENDALL
and WERNER THOMAS

CLIMB EV'RY MOUNTAIN

from THE SOUND OF MUSIC

VIOLA

Lyrics by OSCAR HAMMERSTEIN II
Music by RICHARD RODGERS

Majestically

CRAZY LITTLE THING CALLED LOVE

VIOLA

Words and Music by
FREDDIE MERCURY

COMPLICATED

VIOLA

Words and Music by AVRIL LAVIGNE,
LAUREN CHRISTY, SCOTT SPOCK
and GRAHAM EDWARDS

CROCODILE ROCK

VIOLA

Words and Music by ELTON JOHN
and BERNIE TAUPIN

Upbeat Rock

DANCING QUEEN

VIOLA

Words and Music by BENNY ANDERSSON,
BJORN ULVAEUS and STIG ANDERSON

Strong Rock

DON'T KNOW WHY

VIOLA

Words and Music by
JESSE HARRIS

DREAM LOVER

VIOLA

Words and Music by
BOBBY DARIN

Moderately

DROPS OF JUPITER
(Tell Me)

VIOLA

Words and Music by PAT MONAHAN,
JIMMY STAFFORD, ROB HOTCHKISS,
CHARLIE COLIN and SCOTT UNDERWOOD

D.S. al Coda

CODA

DUST IN THE WIND

VIOLA

Words and Music by
KERRY LIVGREN

EASTER PARADE

from AS THOUSANDS CHEER

VIOLA

Words and Music by
IRVING BERLIN

Moderately

ENDLESS LOVE

VIOLA

Words and Music by
LIONEL RICHIE

FEVER

VIOLA

Words and Music by JOHN DAVENPORT
and EDDIE COOLEY

Moderate Jump beat

FIRE AND RAIN

VIOLA

Words and Music by
JAMES TAYLOR

Slowly

THE FIRST CUT IS THE DEEPEST

VIOLA

Words and Music by
CAT STEVENS

Moderately

THE FOOL ON THE HILL

VIOLA

Words and Music by JOHN LENNON
and PAUL McCARTNEY

FOOTLOOSE
Theme from the Paramount Motion Picture FOOTLOOSE

Words by DEAN PITCHFORD
and KENNY LOGGINS
Music by KENNY LOGGINS

VIOLA

Fast Rock

FROM A DISTANCE

VIOLA

Words and Music by
JULIE GOLD

GO AWAY, LITTLE GIRL

VIOLA

Words and Music by GERRY GOFFIN
and CAROLE KING

Moderately slow

GOOD VIBRATIONS

VIOLA

Words and Music by BRIAN WILSON
and MIKE LOVE

Light Rock

GOT MY MIND SET ON YOU

VIOLA

Words and Music by
RUDY CLARK

A GROOVY KIND OF LOVE

VIOLA

Words and Music by TONI WINE
and CAROLE BAYER SAGER

HAPPY TOGETHER

VIOLA

Words and Music by GARRY BONNER
and ALAN GORDON

HAPPY TRAILS

from the Television Series THE ROY ROGERS SHOW

VIOLA

Words and Music by
DALE EVANS

HEAVEN

VIOLA

Words and Music by BRYAN ADAMS
and JIM VALLANCE

HEAVEN

VIOLA

Words and Music by HENRY GARZA,
JOEY GARZA and RINGO GARZA

HELLO

VIOLA

Words and Music by
LIONEL RICHIE

HIGH HOPES

VIOLA

Words by SAMMY CAHN
Music by JAMES VAN HEUSEN

Moderately, with a beat

HOW CAN YOU MEND A BROKEN HEART

VIOLA

Words and Music by BARRY GIBB
and ROBIN GIBB

HOW SWEET IT IS (TO BE LOVED BY YOU)

VIOLA

Words and Music by EDWARD HOLLAND,
LAMONT DOZIER and BRIAN HOLLAND

I GOT YOU
(I Feel Good)

VIOLA

Words and Music by
JAMES BROWN

(Spoken:) Hey!

I HOPE YOU DANCE

VIOLA

Words and Music by TIA SILLERS
and MARK D. SANDERS

I JUST CALLED TO SAY I LOVE YOU

VIOLA

Words and Music by
STEVIE WONDER

I LEFT MY HEART IN SAN FRANCISCO

VIOLA

Words by DOUGLASS CROSS
Music by GEORGE CORY

Moderately

I SHOT THE SHERIFF

VIOLA

Words and Music by
BOB MARLEY

Moderately slow, with a beat

I WANT TO HOLD YOUR HAND

VIOLA

Words and Music by JOHN LENNON
PAUL McCARTNEY

Moderately, with a beat

I'LL BE THERE

VIOLA

Words and Music by BERRY GORDY,
HAL DAVIS, WILLIE HUTCH
and BOB WEST

I'LL BE

VIOLA

Words and Music by
EDWIN McCAIN

Gently

I'M WITH YOU

VIOLA

Words and Music by AVRIL LAVIGNE, LAUREN CHRISTY,
SCOTT SPOCK and GRAHAM EDWARDS

IF

VIOLA

Words and Music by
DAVID GATES

Moderately, with feeling

IF I HAD A HAMMER
(The Hammer Song)

VIOLA

Words and Music by LEE HAYS
and PETE SEEGER

Moderately

THE IMPRESSION THAT I GET

VIOLA

Words and Music by DICKY BARRETT
and JOE GITTLEMAN

IN THE MOOD

VIOLA

By JOE GARLAND

IT'S A SMALL WORLD

from "it's a small world" at Disneyland Park and Magic Kingdom Park

VIOLA

Words and Music by RICHARD M. SHERMAN
and ROBERT B. SHERMAN

IT'S TOO LATE

VIOLA

Words and Music by CAROLE KING
and TONI STERN

ITSY BITSY TEENIE WEENIE
YELLOW POLKADOT BIKINI

VIOLA

Words and Music by PAUL VANCE
and LEE POCKRISS

THEME FROM "JURASSIC PARK"

from the Universal Motion Picture JURASSIC PARK

VIOLA

Composed by
JOHN WILLIAMS

KING OF THE ROAD

VIOLA

Words and Music by
ROGER MILLER

LA BAMBA

VIOLA

By RITCHIE VALENS

LET IT BE

VIOLA

Words and Music by JOHN LENNON
PAUL McCARTNEY

To Coda ⊕

D.S. al Coda

CODA

⊕

LISTEN TO WHAT THE MAN SAID

VIOLA

Words and Music by
PAUL and LINDA McCARTNEY

THE LOCO-MOTION

VIOLA

Words and Music by GERRY GOFFIN
and CAROLE KING

LOUIE, LOUIE

VIOLA

Words and Music by
RICHARD BERRY

LOVE ME TENDER

VIOLA

Words and Music by ELVIS PRESLEY
and VERA MATSON

Moderately slow

LUCY IN THE SKY WITH DIAMONDS

VIOLA

Words and Music by JOHN LENNON
and PAUL McCARTNEY

MAMBO NO. 5
(A Little Bit Of...)

VIOLA

Original Music by DAMASO PEREZ PRADO
Words by LOU BEGA and ZIPPY

Relaxed two-beat feel

ME AND BOBBY McGEE

VIOLA

Words and Music by KRIS KRISTOFFERSON
and FRED FOSTER

A MOMENT LIKE THIS

VIOLA

Words and Music by JOHN REID
and JORGEN KJELL ELOFSSON

MY FAVORITE THINGS
from THE SOUND OF MUSIC

VIOLA

Lyrics by OSCAR HAMMERSTEIN II
Music by RICHARD RODGERS

Lively, with spirit

THE ODD COUPLE

Theme from the Paramount Picture THE ODD COUPLE
Theme from the Paramount Television Series THE ODD COUPLE

VIOLA

By NEAL HEFTI

ON TOP OF SPAGHETTI

VIOLA

Words and Music by
TOM GLAZER

Moderately fast, with spirit

100 YEARS

VIOLA

Words and Music by
JOHN ONDRASIK

ONE NOTE SAMBA
(Samba de uma nota so)

VIOLA

Original Lyrics by NEWTON MENDONCA
English Lyrics by ANTONIO CARLOS JOBIM
Music by ANTONIO CARLOS JOBIM

Samba

PETER COTTONTAIL

VIOLA

Words and Music by STEVE NELSON
and JACK ROLLINS

Moderately

PUPPY LOVE

VIOLA

Words and Music by
PAUL ANKA

Moderately slow

QUE SERA, SERA
(Whatever Will Be, Will Be)
from THE MAN WHO KNEW TOO MUCH

VIOLA

Words and Music by JAY LIVINGSTON
and RAY EVANS

Moderately bright

R.O.C.K. IN THE U.S.A
(A Salute to 60's Rock)

VIOLA

Words and Music by
JOHN MELLENCAMP

Fast Rock

THE RAINBOW CONNECTION
from THE MUPPET MOVIE

VIOLA

Words and Music by PAUL WILLIAMS
and KENNETH L. ASCHER

Flowing Waltz tempo

RAINDROPS KEEP FALLIN' ON MY HEAD

from BUTCH CASSIDY AND THE SUNDANCE KID

VIOLA

Lyric by HAL DAVID
Music by BURT BACHARACH

ROCKIN' ROBIN

VIOLA

Words and Music by
J. THOMAS

SAILING

VIOLA

Words and Music by
CHRISTOPHER CROSS

Moderately

SEE YOU LATER, ALLIGATOR

VIOLA

Words and Music by
ROBERT GUIDRY

Medium Shuffle (♩♩ = ♩♪)

SEVENTY SIX TROMBONES
from Meredith Willson's THE MUSIC MAN

VIOLA

By MEREDITH WILLSON

SHAKE, RATTLE AND ROLL

VIOLA

Words and Music by
CHARLES CALHOUN

SHOUT

VIOLA

Words and Music by ROLAND ORZABAL
and IAN STANLEY

SIXTEEN GOING ON SEVENTEEN

from THE SOUND OF MUSIC

VIOLA

Lyrics by OSCAR HAMMERSTEIN II
Music by RICHARD RODGERS

SMOOTH

VIOLA

Words by ROB THOMAS
Music by ROB THOMAS and ITALL SHUR

Medium Latin Rock

SO NICE
(Summer Samba)

VIOLA

Original Words and Music by MARCOS VALLE
and PAULO SERGIO VALLE
English Words by NORMAN GIMBEL

Moderately

THE SOUND OF MUSIC
from THE SOUND OF MUSIC

VIOLA

Lyrics by OSCAR HAMMERSTEIN II
Music by RICHARD RODGERS

With much expression

SPINNING WHEEL

VIOLA

Words and Music by
DAVID CLAYTON THOMAS

Funky, moderate Rock

SPLISH SPLASH

VIOLA

Words and Music by BOBBY DARIN
and MURRAY KAUFMAN

With a beat

STAND BY ME

VIOLA

Words and Music by JERRY LEIBER,
MIKE STOLLER and BEN E. KING

Moderately, with a beat

Sunny

VIOLA

Words and Music by
BOBBY HEBB

SUPERCALIFRAGILISTICEXPIALIDOCIOUS

from Walt Disney's MARY POPPINS

VIOLA

Words and Music by RICHARD M. SHERMAN
and ROBERT B. SHERMAN

Brightly

SURFIN' U.S.A.

VIOLA

Words and Music by
CHUCK BERRY

TAKIN' CARE OF BUSINESS

VIOLA

Words and Music by
RANDY BACHMAN

Moderate Rock

TEARS IN HEAVEN

VIOLA

Words and Music by ERIC CLAPTON
and WILL JENNINGS

TENNESSEE WALTZ

VIOLA

Words and Music by REDD STEWART
and PEE WEE KING

THAT'LL BE THE DAY

VIOLA

Words and Music by JERRY ALLISON,
NORMAN PETTY and BUDDY HOLLY

THIS LOVE

VIOLA

Words and Music by ADAM LEVINE
and JESSE CARMICHAEL

Moderate Rock

TIE A YELLOW RIBBON
ROUND THE OLE OAK TREE

VIOLA

Words and Music by L. RUSSELL BROWN
and IRWIN LEVINE

Moderately bright

TIJUANA TAXI

VIOLA

Words by JOHNNY FLAMINGO
Music by ERVAN "BUD" COLEMAN

TRUE COLORS

VIOLA

Words and Music by BILLY STEINBERG
and TOM KELLY

THE TWIST

VIOLA

Words and Music by
HANK BALLARD

UP WHERE WE BELONG

from the Paramount Picture AN OFFICER AND A GENTLEMAN

VIOLA

Words by WILL JENNINGS
Music by BUFFY SAINTE-MARIE and JACK NITZSCHE

WALKING IN MEMPHIS

VIOLA

Words and Music by
MARC COHN

CODA 1

D.S. al Coda 1

Suddenly slowly, freely

Tempo I

2

D.C. al Coda 2

CODA 2

THE WAY YOU LOOK TONIGHT

from SWING TIME

VIOLA

Words by DOROTHY FIELDS
Music by JEROME KERN

WE ARE FAMILY

VIOLA

Words and Music by NILE RODGERS
and BERNARD EDWARDS

Dance tempo

WE ARE THE CHAMPIONS

VIOLA

Words and Music by
FREDDIE MERCURY

Moderately slow

WE BUILT THIS CITY

VIOLA

Words and Music by BERNIE TAUPIN, MARTIN PAGE,
DENNIS LAMBERT and PETER WOLF

WE'VE ONLY JUST BEGUN

VIOLA

Words and Music by ROGER NICHOLS
and PAUL WILLIAMS

WHITE FLAG

VIOLA

Words and Music by RICK NOWELS,
ROLLO ARMSTRONG and DIDO ARMSTRONG

Moderately slow

A WHOLE NEW WORLD

from Walt Disney's ALADDIN

VIOLA

Music by ALAN MENKEN
Lyrics by TIM RICE

Y.M.C.A.

VIOLA

Words and Music by JACQUES MORALI,
HENRI BELOLO and VICTOR WILLIS

Yesterday

VIOLA

Words and Music by JOHN LENNON
and PAUL McCARTNEY

Moderately, with expression

YOU ARE MY SUNSHINE

VIOLA

Words and Music by
JIMMIE DAVIS

YOU LIGHT UP MY LIFE

VIOLA

Words and Music by
JOSEPH BROOKS

Moderately slow

YOU ARE THE MUSIC IN ME

from the Disney Channel Original Movie HIGH SCHOOL MUSICAL 2

VIOLA

Words and Music by
JAMIE HOUSTON

Moderately fast Rock

YOU'RE BEAUTIFUL

VIOLA

Words and Music by JAMES BLUNT,
SACHA SKARBEK and AMANDA GHOST

YOU'RE STILL THE ONE

VIOLA

Words and Music by SHANIA TWAIN
and ROBERT JOHN LANGE

Slowly

YOU'VE GOT A FRIEND IN ME

from Walt Disney's TOY STORY

VIOLA

Music and Lyrics by
RANDY NEWMAN

YOUR SONG

VIOLA

Words and Music by ELTON JOHN
and BERNIE TAUPIN

ZOOT SUIT RIOT

VIOLA

Words and Music by
STEVE PERRY

Spoken: *Blow, dad-dy!*